The 4 Cuties – Freundinnen

Finale

Part x

For my husband

Author Cover Images
Tanja M. Feiler

1. The 3 Cutiesongs

The Cutiesong

The 4 Cuties

are the best

friends yes

they running in the land

hand in hand

hand in hand

running in the land

the 4 cuties are the best

The new Cutiesong

Sing the Cutiesong

All time long

yes with yeppa say JAAA

Cuties on the world

singing a word

with the song

all time long

Sing the Cutiesong

All time long Yes with yeppa
say JAAA

Where are the cuties?

Beginning with one
3000 girls with fun
cuties everywhere
are there

Wo sind die Cuties
sie sind lucky

Everybody can do

what to do

in his own house

Wo sind die Cuties

sie sind lucky

Understanding or not

they are hot

all sisters by me

cuties I see

ps: I love you

2. The Revolution

The 4 Cuties - girlfriends came out of the idea to learn about therapeutic help based on field research. The field research is based on the experience of the Creator 4 Cuties - girlfriends. You slip into the next volumes 1-9 in the roles of therapists, stylists, photographers, these are their professions, they perform with passion.   Psychologically,

middle - the creeping
revolution with the question:
life with one or four women -
or with lots in a pyramid?

3. Finale

In the last part the girlfriends see the pyramid and pictures about the ideas of creating the rooms of the pyramid. They understand, that perhaps many girls live together with the 4 cuties – and that made trouble.

They present some of their pictures of the Make – up Colleciton

17

They are very proud of their diffrent collections. They made some new images with their diamont Collection. Here are the best of them:

Diamond

Besonders Danke ich meinem
Ehemann

www.ingramcontent.com/pod-product-compliance
Lightning Source LLC
Chambersburg PA
CBHW050933290526
45792CB00002B/993